OUR CHANGING WEATHER

Cumulus clouds on a summer afternoon. Wind has broken a few of the clouds, making them fracto-cumulus.

1900—

By CARROLL LANE FENTON and MILDRED ADAMS FENTON

OUR CHANGING WEATHER

DOUBLEDAY & COMPANY, INC., GARDEN CITY, NEW YORK

Contents

Our Changing Weather   7

What Makes the Weather?   9

How the Earth Causes Seasons   12

Air and the Atmosphere   17

Light and Warmth from the Sun   21

Heat and How It Works   26

Air Travels Around the Earth   28

Some Local Winds   33

Land, Water, and Weather   38

Water in the Air   42

Clouds of Various Kinds   46

Haze, Fogs, and Rain   57

Thunderstorms and Lightning   63

Snowflakes and Snowstorms   68

Dew and Frost   73

Where Weather Comes From   77

How Air Masses Change   82

What Happens on Fronts   87

Storms That Whirl   92

Cyclones, Lows, and Highs   98

Reading the Weather Map   103

Making Our Own Forecasts   108

This high mountain makes moisture in the air form clouds from which rain will soon fall.

Our Changing Weather

Have you ever wished you could change the weather? Would you like to turn rainy days into dry ones, or cold days into days that are warm? Do you want to bring snow at Christmas time, or stir up a breeze to fly your kite on a quiet afternoon in the spring?

You can't do these things, of course, yet something does make the weather change over and over again. Suppose a day starts out dull and damp. Clouds cover the sky and raindrops soon begin to fall. Harder and faster they come, until people who go outdoors get wet, even though they wear raincoats and rubbers and carry their umbrellas.

The rain may last a long time, but finally it comes to an end. The wind begins to blow fast, or hard, and patches of sky appear between broken, ragged-looking clouds. Then some of the broken clouds disappear, and the sky becomes blue instead of dull gray. As the color of the sky changes, the sun shines brightly upon the rain-soaked land.

Hour after hour goes by, and the weather keeps on changing. The wind turns into a gentle breeze, and clouds begin to look like balls of fluffy cotton. Perhaps the air turns crisp and cool, or perhaps it becomes so warm that we want to sit in the shade and rest.

All these changes come without our help, and we can't slow them down or hurry them up. If we don't understand them or know why they are coming, we also may get into trouble. We may plan picnics on days that are sure to be rainy, or we may wear thin, hot-weather clothing on days that are going to turn cool. We may also give up trips and stay indoors on days that become just right for hikes or automobile rides.

Although we can't change the weather, we can do something else. We can find out what the different kinds of weather are like, what makes them and why they follow each other. When we learn these whats and whys, we shall understand rain, snow, sunshine, clouds, fine weather, and storms. We shall also understand the weather forecasts that come by radio and television or are published in newspapers. Best of all, we can make our own forecasts from clouds, winds, and the "feel" of the air. These forecasts will not be quite so good as those made by the weather man, but they will get better as we keep on trying. In time, we may even make a few forecasts that come out right when the weather man is wrong!

It is fun to find out for ourselves what kind of weather is coming late today or tomorrow. It also is the next best thing to changing the weather, so it will be just what we want.

EARTH + AIR + HEAT + WATER = WEATHE[R]

What Makes the Weather?

"Such weather! What in the world makes it?"

You hear people say things like this on rainy days, windy days, and days that are very cold. But can you answer their questions? Can you tell what makes the weather, no matter what it is like?

The best way to find out what makes the weather is to watch it for a day. Take the day we have just described, if you like. It started out with dampness and clouds, which soon sent down rain. Then the rain stopped and wind began to blow, tearing the clouds to pieces and driving them across the sky. At last the day became clear and dry, and the air moved so slowly that we called it a gentle breeze.

As we trace these changes, we pick out several great weather-makers. The first one, of course, is air. Air carries clouds and takes them away; it brings heat waves or cold spells, and it helps to cause thunderstorms. In fact, air helps produce every kind of weather in every part of the world.

9

The second great weather-maker is heat. Heat makes sunny days warmer than days that are cloudy. It makes summer weather warmer than winter weather, too, and provides the warmth of hot spells. Heat also makes many winds blow, sends water into the air, and even starts thunderstorms.

Our third great weather-maker is water, which we often call moisture. Water goes into the air, or evaporates, from oceans, lakes, rivers, and even from the ground. Some of this water soon forms clouds, from which rain or snow may fall. Water also stays in the air, in tiny bits, or particles, which are much

The earth makes the weather in this valley so dry that only a few plants can grow, while sand is blown into hills called dunes.

too small to be seen. Air that contains some water is pleasant, but air that contains a great deal is humid (hew′ mid). We often call humid weather "muggy," and it feels just as bad as it sounds.

Some people say that these are the only great weather-makers, but there really is one more. It is a huge ball, and we see its surface every day. It gets all kinds of weather, and it helps make every one.

This fourth great weather-maker is the earth. We shall find that the earth helps air and heat produce winds, and makes some of them blow very hard. The earth also causes the difference between summer and winter, and it forces many clouds to turn into rain or snow. Finally, the earth's surface sends cool, moist weather to some places, but makes others warm and dry. At this very moment, the earth may be sending fog or drizzle over your home, although the weather is bright and sunny only a few miles away.

Earth, air, heat, and water: these are the four great weather-makers. Now that we know what they are, let's find out more about them and about the kinds of weather which they make.

How the Earth Causes Seasons

Some deserts have hot weather every day but are cold at night. In other places the weather changes just as much but not so fast. One day may be hot and the next one cool. Rainy times are followed by droughts. Heat waves come after cool weather and rain.

There is a big difference between a hot day and a chilly night, or between rains and droughts. But in many parts of the world, the greatest weather changes come as season follows season.

Shall we find out why there are seasons, and why they bring different weather? To do this, let's take an imaginary space ship and sail far into the sky. There we cruise about, watching the earth and the sun.

As we look through the windows of our space ship, we see that the earth turns round and round. It does so upon its axis, which is an imaginary line that runs through the North Pole and the South Pole. Instead of pointing up and down, this line is tilted to one side.

While the earth turns upon its axis, it travels around the sun. It goes in a path called its orbit, which is almost a circle. The orbit is so big that the earth takes a year to make one full trip around it.

Suppose we watch the earth as it goes. We begin on a day late in June, when the tilted axis makes the North Pole point toward the sun. This lets sunshine fall on the Pole and beyond. It also makes days longer than nights on the northern half of the earth, called the northern hemisphere. Long days of sunlight bring warm weather and tell us that summer has come.

Week after week the earth keeps on going. Since the axis always slants in the same direction, the North Pole soon begins to turn away from the sun. Daytime becomes shorter in the northern hemisphere, and nights become longer. Three months after the beginning of summer, day and night are of just the same length. This is the time when fall, or autumn, begins.

Autumn also lasts three months, until winter begins in December. Now the North Pole points away from the sun, and it gets no light except from the

How the seasons change as our earth travels round the sun.

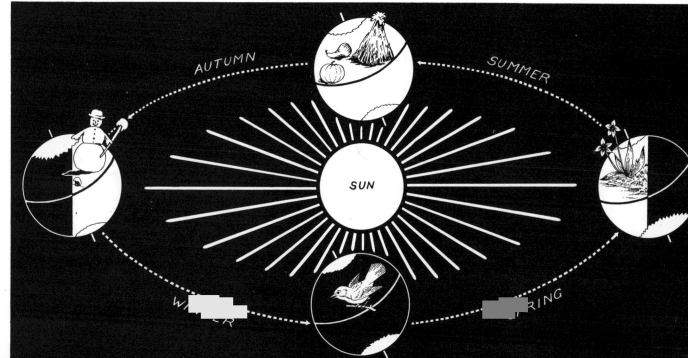

moon and the stars. In the rest of the northern hemisphere, day is shorter than night. The weather becomes cooler, too. In many places it grows so cold that water freezes into ice and snow covers the ground.

On and on goes the earth, until it is opposite the place where it was when autumn began. Day and night become equal again, and the weather turns warmer, as it always does when spring begins. In three more months the earth completes its trip. The North Pole now points towards the sun, which means that summer has come again to the northern hemisphere.

Seasons on the southern half of the earth are just the opposite of ours. The southern winter begins near the end of June, when the South Pole points farthest away from the sun. Spring starts when autumn comes to the North. December brings the beginning of summer, for that is when the South Pole points farthest toward the sun.

_____

Days are longest in summer and shortest in winter. But why should summer be warmer than winter? Does the earth come close to the sun when weather is hot and go farther away when it turns cold?

That would be an easy explanation, but it would not be right. The earth actually is about three million miles closer to the sun when winter begins than it is on the first day of summer. If distance made weather warm or cool, summer would be the chilliest season.

One real reason why summer is warmer than winter is the fact that summer days are long. The sun rises early and sets late, and for fourteen or fifteen hours it warms our hemisphere. Heat "piles up" in air and water, in buildings,

Rays from our flashlight sun are crowded, or concentrated, in "summer" but spread out in the "winter" part of our experiment.

and in the ground. This often makes the weather so hot that plants wilt, birds hide in trees, and people who work out of doors take special care to keep from becoming sick.

This does not happen during the winter, when the sun rises late and sets early. Since it shines only eight or ten hours, it does not have time to make the weather hot.

Summer also is warmer than winter because the sun makes more heat in one season than it does in the other.

Summer comes to our half of the earth when the North Pole points toward the sun. This lets sunlight fall directly on air, land, and water, and its rays make a great deal of heat. But when winter comes, the North Pole is tipped in the opposite direction, and sunlight falls at a slant. The slanting rays spread out, making so little heat that the weather becomes chilly or cold.

15

We can tell just how this happens by making two experiments with a piece of white paper and a flashlight. First we put the paper on the floor of a dark room and shine the flashlight directly down upon it, as the sun shines on our earth in the summer. The light makes a small circle, in which rays are crowded, or concentrated. If they were heating the paper, they would make it very warm.

Next we hold the flashlight at a slant, as the sun shines in winter. The flashlight sends out the same number of rays, but they spread out in an oval of light that is much larger than the circle. If those rays were heating the paper, they would not make it nearly so warm as the rays that were crowded together in the "summer" part of our experiment.

———

There is one part of our earth, called the Tropics, where the weather is not much cooler in winter than it is in summertime. The Tropics lie on both sides of the equator, which is an imaginary line that divides the northern and southern hemispheres. This part of the earth is so far from the poles that it never tips much one way or the other. Winter days are almost as long as days in the summer, and sunshine comes almost "straight down" during every season. That is why tropical weather does not change much as our earth goes round the sun.

Air and the Atmosphere

As we look down on the earth from our space ship, we notice the atmosphere. It looks like a coat of haze, with white patches, that covers our whirling planet.

We say that the atmosphere "covers" the earth, but that is not quite true. The atmosphere actually is the outermost part of our ball-shaped world. It begins at the surfaces of lands and seas, and goes up at least 700 miles. Instead of living on top of the earth, we really make our homes under 700 miles of atmosphere.

We may *notice* the atmosphere from our space ship, but we do not *see* it. For the atmosphere is made of air, and air is a mixture of gases that have no color and are much too thin to be seen. We notice this mixture because it contains clouds, dust, and tiny particles of water. They reflect sunlight, making the atmosphere look hazy, with patches of white that are clouds.

Since the atmosphere is very thick, it also is very heavy. The air above one square inch of sea or lowland weighs almost 15 pounds. If your hand is five inches long and three inches wide, the atmosphere pushes against it with a weight of about 200 pounds.

You don't feel this weight because air pushes upward against your hand as hard as it pushes downward. Air pushes against all sides of your body, too, and it presses against the inside of cans, automobiles, and houses as hard as it pushes against the outside. Houses explode when storms called tornadoes make outside air push much less than air inside hallways and rooms.

If we put 200 pounds on a stone one inch square, nothing seems to happen. But since air is not hard, like a stone, it can be squeezed together, or compressed. When we stand on low ground or on the seashore, we are in air that is compressed by those 200 pounds of weight above every square inch of surface. This makes air near the ground much thicker, or denser, than it is high up in the atmosphere.

We find this out when we climb a high mountain, for the air becomes so thin that we gasp for breath. If we go to the top of a mountain 18,000 feet high, we find that half of the air in the atmosphere has been squeezed into the space below us. At 35,000 feet (almost seven miles), the air above one square inch weighs only 4 pounds. This thin air blows in very strong winds and is very, very cold, even on the brightest, hottest summer days.

Many things happen to our weather because air can be either thick or thin and because most thin air turns cold. Other things happen because air moves about, going to and fro and up and down inside the atmosphere.

Most of these things happen in a "shell" of air called the *troposphere* (trop′ o sfeer), which begins at sea level and goes upward seven to eight miles. *Tropo* means change, and almost all our changing weather comes in this part of the atmosphere.

The *tropopause* (trop′ o paws) is a layer of very thin, cold air above the troposphere. Most changes stop in this layer, though winds blow day after day at speeds of 150, 200, or 300 miles per hour.

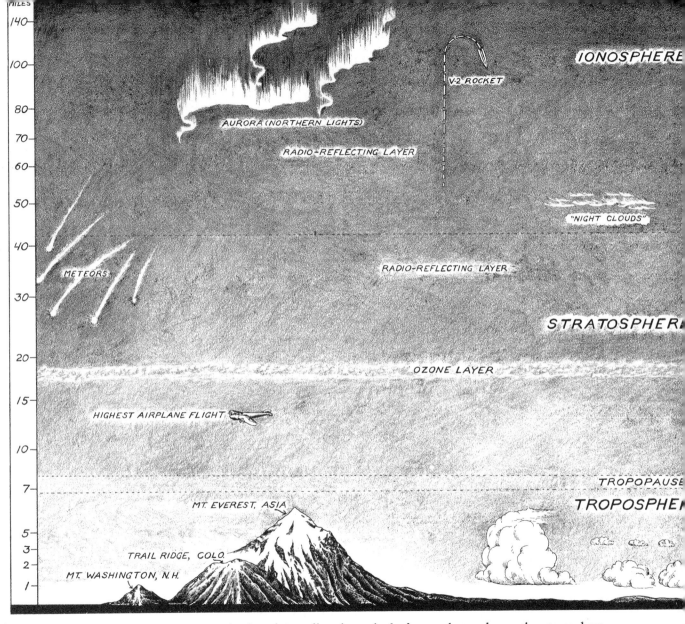

An imaginary slice through the layers that make up the atmosphere.

The *stratosphere* (stray' toe sfeer) begins about 9 miles up and goes to a height of 40 or 45 miles. Most of the stratosphere is cold, but a layer that contains a great deal of gas called *ozone* (oe' zone) is much warmer than air near the ground. Another layer reflects radio waves, sending them back to the surface of lands and seas. Most meteors become bright and burn up in the stratosphere. It also contains clouds of very fine dust or ice crystals, which sometimes glow with reflected sunlight at night, long after the sky is dark near the ground.

Only rockets can go through the stratosphere and into the *ionosphere* (eye on' o sfeer), which begins 40 to 45 miles above the ground and goes to a height of about 700 miles. The northern lights, or aurora, appear in the ionosphere. It also contains a layer that sends radio waves back to the ground, but so far as we know, this layer does not have much effect on our weather.

Light and Warmth from the Sun

In springtime the air becomes warm. It melts snow in the North and upon high mountains. It makes plants grow and bloom and sets insects to humming among flowers. The warm air makes us feel good, too, if we live where the winter has been cold.

We sometimes say that the sun sends heat to the earth, but that is not quite true. The sun sends out rays of energy, which travel through space like waves that ripple over water. They go faster than water waves, however, for they take only eight minutes to come all the way from the sun.

All the sun's rays travel at the same speed, but they are not alike. Some have short waves, many have long ones, and others are in between. We call the in-betweens *visible light*, or light that can be seen. The very short waves are ultraviolet, which means "shorter than violet light." Rays with long waves are often called heat waves, since they produce a great deal of heat when they come to the earth.

21

The sun's rays shoot through our atmosphere in one two-hundredth of a second. During that time, many ultraviolet rays are caught by the ozone layer and are turned into heat. They make the ozone layer warmer than air near the ground.

Many rays of visible light strike tiny dust grains, moisture, and particles of gas in the atmosphere and then are thrown back, or reflected. Since most of these reflected rays are blue, they make the sky look blue on bright, sunny days.

Light that is not reflected keeps on traveling through the atmosphere, coming close to the earth's surface or even bumping into it. There many of the rays are reflected from clouds, mountains, plants, and millions of other things. These rays are the light with which we see. They also make pictures on film when we "snap" our cameras.

Light rays that are not reflected stay right where they fall. So do most heat rays, which should really be called heat-makers. As the rays are trapped, or absorbed, the energy which they brought from the sun is turned into actual heat. You can see how this happens in the picture on page 23.

If you could touch one of the rocks in this picture, you would find it very hot. You also would find that some of its heat would travel into your hand. In the same way, when the atmosphere touches warm land or water, heat goes into the air. In the winter it may not have much effect, but when spring comes it warms the weather, and in the summer it often makes the weather very hot.

We know how warm the weather can be around our bodies, up above the ground. It gets still hotter close to soil and rocks, especially in southern deserts, where the sun shines brightly all day. Many lizards, snakes, and insects hide

Rays from the sun are absorbed and turned into heat, which then goes into the air and makes the weather warm.

from morning till evening, but some of them remain active and never seem to hunt for shade. The black beetle shown on this page often runs about in bright sunshine which makes the temperature close to the ground go as high as 200 degrees!

———

The air does not keep, or absorb, many rays. Pure air also does not hold much heat — but air near the ground never is pure. It always contains dust and the gas called carbon dioxide, which makes soda pop "fizz." Air also contains

This lizard and beetle live on the ground in southwestern deserts. There the weather becomes so hot that the lizard has to hide in shade, but the beetle runs about even when the temperature goes to 200 degrees.

tiny particles of water, as well as larger droplets that form haze or clouds. These impurities turn rays into heat, and they keep heat produced on land or in water from going right out into space. This explains why damp air often remains hot at night, long after the sun stops shining. We say that such moist, hot nights are "sultry," and are glad when they come to an end.

We don't like sultry nights, but we do want air to keep some of the heat which it gets from land and water. If the air did not hold heat, our nights would grow terribly cold. Except in the hottest part of the earth, temperatures would probably drop to 100 degrees below zero an hour or two after sunset.

A hundred degrees below zero! Br-rr-rr! That would freeze every plant on the earth's surface and most of the animals. It would break hard rocks to pieces and would make people chilly in the warmest houses. Aren't you glad that the air has impurities which help it catch and hold the heat made from rays that fall upon land and water?

Heat and How It Works

We have found that our earth soaks up, or absorbs, rays from the sun and turns them into heat. But just what is heat? And what happens when heated ground warms the atmosphere?

One way to answer this question is to lay a cool, dark stone in the sunshine on a summer day. Since the stone is dark, it absorbs many light rays, as well as the long, heat-making rays which we cannot see. These rays disappear, but they are not destroyed. Their energy becomes heat that warms the stone and then the air above it.

The picture on page 27 explains this. Although the stone seems to be solid, it actually is made up of tiny lumps called *molecules* (moll' i kewlz), which fit together very loosely with lots of space between them. When the stone is cool, these tiny lumps jiggle to and fro and bump each other, but not very rapidly. We could see them do so if we had a magnifying glass that would make them look 30,000 or 40,000 times larger than they really are.

The magnifying glass also would show what happens when our piece of stone lies in the sunshine. Energy from the sun's rays goes into the molecules, making them move faster and bump harder than they did before. That is what we really mean when we say that the sun's rays are turned into heat, warming the dark stone.

As the sun keeps on shining upon the stone, more and more energy goes into the molecules. This makes them bounce and bump faster and faster, as we can see from dotted lines in the picture. If we touch the stone with our fingers, we discover that it is hot.

Air also touches the stone as it becomes hot. Air is made of molecules, too, but they are so far apart and and move so easily that they form gases, not something solid. When molecules in our stone hit those in the air, the molecules of gas bounce away and begin to bump into each other. This means that the hot stone is now warming the air.

One piece of rock will not make warm spring weather or a hot summer day. But our one stone does not work alone. Everything at the earth's surface absorbs rays and heats the air. This makes days and seasons warm and provides the heat that is needed to change our weather all the year round.

When rays from the sun go into a stone, they make its molecules move faster and faster, which means that the stone becomes hot.

RAYS FROM THE SUN FALL ON A STONE...

...MAKING MOLECULES BOUNCE AND BUMP EACH OTHER

HOT AIR BEGINS TO FILL THE BALLOON

IT GROWS LARGER AND LARGER

AND THEN FLOATS AWAY

A balloon filled with hot air floated in the cooler air around it.

Air Travels Around the Earth

Before airplanes became common, "daring" aviators sometimes went aloft in hot-air balloons. Each balloon was a cloth bag that was filled with hot air from a fire. When the bag could hold no more air, ropes that held it to the ground were loosened and it floated away.

The pictures on page 29 show why a balloon filled with hot air was so light that it floated. Air, as we know, is mostly space in which molecules of gas bounce to and fro. In cool air the molecules bounce slowly and are not very far apart. Sixteen of them are crowded into Picture 1.

Picture 2 shows what happens when the air is heated by a fire, or by warm land and water. Molecules now move faster and hit harder when they bump into each other. This makes them bounce much farther. The second picture is as big as the first, but it has room for only ten molecules.

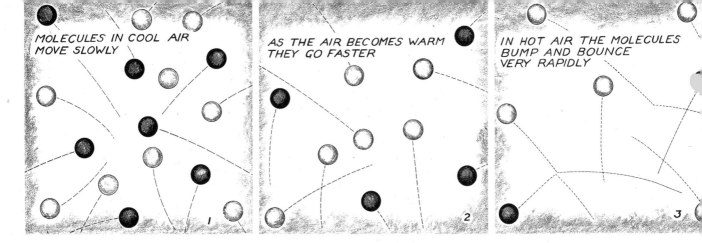

MOLECULES IN COOL AIR MOVE SLOWLY

AS THE AIR BECOMES WARM THEY GO FASTER

IN HOT AIR THE MOLECULES BUMP AND BOUNCE VERY RAPIDLY

As air is heated its molecules bounce so fast that they take up more and more space. This makes hot air weigh less than air that is cool.

The third picture shows the air after it becomes hot. The molecules now move still faster, bump still harder, and bounce still farther. We see only seven of them, instead of ten or sixteen.

You know that ten pennies or marbles weigh less than sixteen, and that seven weigh less than ten. In the same way, hot air that filled a ballon weighed less than the air around it. So the balloon began to float, just as a rubber ball will float if you put it in water.

———

Air outdoors also floats when it grows warm or hot. But instead of going away in balloons, it forms great currents and winds that travel over the earth. We can find out why they do so if we take our make-believe space ship and cruise far away from the earth. We also imagine a special kind of spyglass that will let us see air as well as water and land.

29

The first thing we notice through our spyglass is heated air rising above the equator, where the earth becomes very warm. As the heated air goes upward, air that is not so hot flows in from each side.

So far all is simple — but something else soon happens. As the warm air goes higher and higher, the pressure upon it becomes less and less. This lets molecules spread out so far that they do not bump and bounce very often. When that happens the warm air loses heat and becomes cool again. It also becomes heavy and sinks. In time it comes back to the lands and seas.

If the earth did not turn, air would float (or rise) above the equator and go upward until it became cool. Then the air would slide downhill to the North Pole and the South Pole, and would flow back to the equator again. This would make only two huge air currents, one in each hemisphere.

The earth does turn round and round, of course, once every twenty-four hours. This makes the cooling air drift eastward as it flows toward the poles. It also divides the air into several currents that travel in different directions when they come down to the surface.

With our spyglass we watch the currents made as the moving air divides. The first currents we see form the *trade winds*, which got their name back in the days when *trade* meant "a regular path." Trade winds of the northern hemisphere blow in a regular path from the northeast until they come to the equator, where the air goes upward again. Trade winds in the southern hemisphere always blow from the southeast.

Just north and south of the trade winds, two other currents blow in the opposite direction. These currents make the *prevailing westerlies*, which blow from the southwest or the northwest during a large part of the year. Still, the prevailing westerlies are not as reliable as the trade winds, especially in Canada and the United States. They may blow for days and then stop, or they may be replaced by other winds which we call "local." We shall find out more about local winds on pages 33 to 37.

The last great air currents begin near the North Pole and the South Pole. In our hemisphere, one of these currents makes winds that come from the

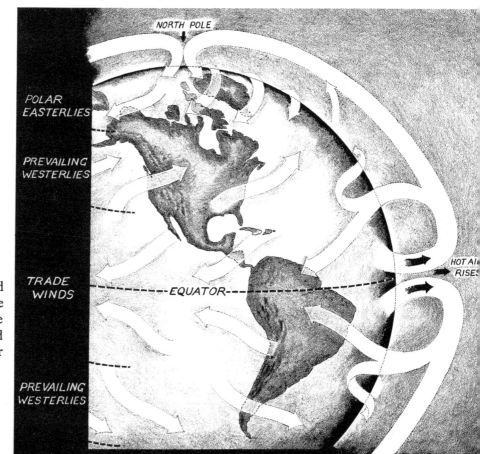

Air near the earth's equator is warmed and rises. Currents formed when the warm air cools and flows back to the surface become several kinds of wind that blow over different parts of our planet.

northeast, and so are called "polar northeasterlies." They blow across Greenland, Alaska, and northern Canada. Polar southeasterly winds are not shown on page 31, but they blow across the continent of Antarctica.

Now that we know why air currents form, we can tell why the weather is cold on high mountains and high up in the troposphere. The air up there is not under much pressure and is lighter, or thinner, than air near lowlands or seas. Molecules are so far apart that they cannot bump into each other very often or bounce very rapidly. That is another way of saying that the air is cold, not warm.

High, thin air also contains less dust, smoke, and moisture than air close to the ground. This means that air over mountain tops cannot hold heat that comes from rocks or soil. They can become hot and send heat into the atmosphere, but it goes out into space instead of warming the air around high ridges and peaks.

HOW HEATED AIR "FLOATS"
AND CAUSES A WIND

HOT A
GOES
UPWA.

COOL AIR (WIND)

Some Local Winds

Suppose, when we get up in the morning, that the prevailing westerly wind is not blowing, and there "isn't a breath of air." There actually is plenty of air, but we do not notice it because it is not moving. It is so still, or calm, that smoke from chimneys goes straight upward and flags hang limply from poles.

Soon — perhaps while we are eating breakfast — the air begins to move. It carries smoke sidewise and makes flags flap lazily. As the air moves faster, branches sway, flags wave, and papers blow along city streets. At last the air goes so fast that it bends treetops, drives smoke away from chimneys, and whips flags to and fro.

We already know why this happens. At first, air near the ground is as cool at one place as another, so it does not move. But the sun sends down rays that are turned into heat, which warms air in some places more than it does in others. This makes pockets of warm, light-weight air that begin to rise.

33

Soon they flow upward in steady streams which we call *convection* (kon-vek′ shun) currents, while cool air near the ground takes their place. This causes a sidewise flow of air — and that is another way to say *wind*.

Winds that form in this way generally blow all day. They also may become very strong, especially on plains in the West, where trees and hills do not get in their way. But when evening comes the winds "die down," for the land no longer heats the air and makes it rise rapidly. The winds stop blowing soon after sunset, letting the air become as calm as it was early in the morning.

Suppose we now leave the plains and take a trip to some high mountains. What kind of winds blow there?

In mountain valleys, on summer days, the air often becomes very warm. It grows lighter and begins to rise, but it does not go straight upward. Instead, it flows up the valleys, making breezes that sometimes go all the way to the tops of ridges and peaks.

These breezes stop soon after sunset, and new ones begin to blow. They are made of air that covers high places, where it cools and becomes heavy. As soon as the sun goes down and breezes of warm air stop blowing uphill, this cool air begins to flow downward. When it gets into valleys it blows along slowly, making chilly breezes.

Other mountain winds blow in the daytime, faster than they blow at night. This often happens when sheets, or masses, of air that are many miles wide travel over mountain ranges. Air climbs up slopes, comes to the top, and starts downhill. Often it goes slowly, but sometimes it blows in high winds or

Winds that blow up the side of a mountain have bent this tree, making its trunk grow on the ground. Trees such as this are said to be "wind-sheared."

A chinook wind becomes warm as it travels down the sides of mountains. This chinook becomes 30 degrees warmer than the air around high, cool peaks.

gales that howl across slopes, rush through valleys, and stir up waves on lakes. The rushing wind also breaks twigs and branches from trees and bends others so far that their trunks grow along the ground. When you see such trees you may be sure that winds often blow very hard.

The strangest mountain winds of all are called *chinooks* (shi nooks'). A chinook begins as warm, moist air that crosses high mountain ranges. As the air goes up it expands and cools, and most of the moisture in it turns into rain or snow. At the top of the mountains, the air starts downhill. As it goes, its molecules are pressed together so hard that they bump and bounce and make the air warm. If the air slides downhill 5,000 feet it becomes 30 degrees warmer than it was on the mountain top.

Suppose the air in a chinook wind is only 10 degrees below freezing (22 degrees above zero) when it goes over the tops of some mountains. Down it goes for almost a mile, becoming 6 degrees warmer in every thousand feet. When the wind gets out of the mountains, its temperature is 20 degrees *above* freezing, or 52 degrees above zero. The warmed-up air melts snow that covers the ground and makes winter days as warm as spring. If the chinook comes right after a "cold snap," it may make the weather 40 degrees warmer in fifteen or twenty minutes!

Chinook winds are commonest east of the Rocky Mountains, but winds that are warmed as they go downhill also blow near the Pacific coast and in the eastern part of North America. When cold air that comes from the northwest crosses the Appalachian Mountains, it slides downhill and is warmed as much as 10 or 15 degrees. This is one reason why weather near the Atlantic coast never becomes as cold as it does in the central part of our country, where there are no mountains.

AIR IS COOLED AND FLOWS DOWNWARD

AIR HEATED OVER THE LAND RISES

COOL AIR FLOWS TO THE LAND

How an onshore breeze develops on a hot summer day.

Land, Water, and Weather

In the summer we like to go to the seacoast or to the shores of big lakes. The water always feels cool, and the weather never becomes so hot as it does on land.

We know that weather becomes hot on the land because soil and rocks turn the sun's rays into heat. This heat stays close to the surface, where most of it warms the air.

Lakes and seas turn rays into heat, too, but it does not stay at the surface. Some heat is quickly lost when water evaporates. Waves and currents also mix the water, taking heat downward much faster than it goes downward on land. This keeps the surface from becoming warm enough to send much heat into the air. That is why winds that blow over water on summer days feel cool instead of hot.

If we stand on a hill close to the shore, we may watch a cool breeze develop. First, of course, comes sunshine on land, which warms some air so much that it goes up in a convection current. This lets cool air begin to travel sidewise. It rustles leaves and makes flags flutter, showing that a breeze is now blowing from the sea or lake.

This *onshore breeze* becomes stronger as the land grows hot. Heated air also rises so high that its molecules spread out and become cool. The cool air goes back over the water, where it comes down to the surface and blows toward the land again.

Round and round goes the air, cooling the lakeshore or seacoast. But when night comes there is a change. The onshore breeze stops blowing, and an *offshore breeze* begins to blow from the land to the sea.

This change comes because the sun has stopped shining, and the land gets no more rays which make its surface hot. The land loses heat, or cools off, faster

An offshore breeze begins to blow when air above the land is cooled at night.

AIR WARMED OVER THE
WATER RISES

AIR COOLED
OVER THE LAND
GOES DOWN

COOLED AIR NOW BLOWS
OVER THE WATER

than water does. As this happens, air above the ground also cools and begins to sink. But air over the water still gets some of the heat that was stored away during the daytime. This makes the "sea air" rise and lets cool air come from the land in the offshore breeze.

———

Changes much like these also come as one season follows another. In summer, air that comes from the sea or a big lake feels cool, and it keeps the weather on nearby land from becoming very hot. But when winter comes and the land grows cool, air that blows across the water still gets a small amount

Why land heats the air more than water does on a summer day. The wriggly black arrows represent heat going into the air.

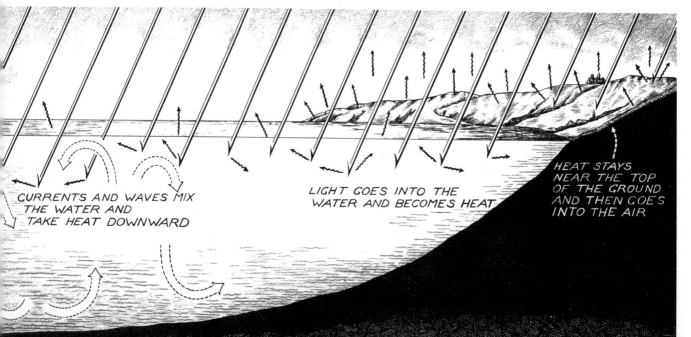

CURRENTS AND WAVES MIX THE WATER AND TAKE HEAT DOWNWARD

LIGHT GOES INTO THE WATER AND BECOMES HEAT

HEAT STAYS NEAR THE TOP OF THE GROUND AND THEN GOES INTO THE AIR

of heat. This makes weather near the shore milder than it is far away from the coast.

We see how important this is if we go from a place near the ocean to one that is far inland. Eastport, Maine, for example, is a city on the seashore. Its average temperature in January is 21 degrees above zero, though some days are 23 below. Glendive, Montana, is no farther north than Eastport, but is 900 miles from the ocean. Since Glendive gets no sea air, its winter temperatures go as low as 50 degrees below zero, and they average only 14 above. But when July comes, Glendive's average is 13 degrees warmer than Eastport. Some days are 117 in the shade, though air from the ocean has never let Eastport get hotter than 93 degrees.

Warm currents that flow through the sea make still bigger differences. The Gulf Stream, for example, is a current of warm water that starts out near Florida, crosses the Atlantic Ocean, and flows past the British Isles. They are as far north as central Canada, and we might expect them to get very cold. Actually, the weather in southern England is a good deal like weather in San Francisco. The coldest day in London was 4 degrees *above* zero, but a Canadian town that is no farther north sometimes has temperatures of 54 degrees *below!*

Water in the Air

On stormy days, clouds often separate and let the sun shine through. It sends its bright rays down to the earth. We sometimes say the sun is "drawing water" from lowlands, lakes, or seas. Actually, the sun shines upon dust and billions of water droplets that already are in the air. These things reflect the sunshine, making streaks of light called *crepuscular* (kri pus' kew lar) rays which show against the cloudy sky. Similar streaks (anti-crepuscular rays) sometimes shine upward when the sun is setting.

Do you know how droplets of water get into the air where the sun can shine upon them? Can you tell how they change again and again, and what they do to the weather?

42

These anti-crepuscular rays are made by sunlight that shines on dust and droplets of water in the air.

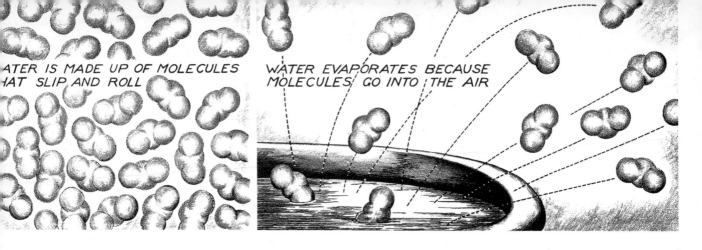

WATER IS MADE UP OF MOLECULES THAT SLIP AND ROLL

WATER EVAPORATES BECAUSE MOLECULES GO INTO THE AIR

A good way to begin this story is to fill a wide, shallow pan with water and set it outdoors in the sunshine. Soon the water begins to go away, or evaporate. In a few days it disappears, leaving the pan empty.

Water evaporates because it is not what it seems to be. It seems to be a thin, "runny" liquid that has no pieces or parts. Actually, water is made up of molecules, just like stones, air, and every other thing on earth. Instead of sticking tightly together, water molecules roll and slip past each other very easily. This explains why water is not solid, and why it "runs" or pours.

When rays from the sun fall upon water, part of them are reflected, but more are turned into heat. Heat makes the molecules roll and slip still faster, until they begin to bounce. At last they bounce out of the pan and float away in the air. The floating molecules are water vapor, which is one kind of gas.

Water evaporates all the time, sending vapor into the air from rivers, lakes, and seas, as well as from swamps and marshes. Water vapor comes from moist soil, too, and from trees, weeds, and other plants that grow on the ground. Even ice and snow evaporate, and their molecules bounce away into the air above them.

All this means that there is water vapor everywhere—in the air outdoors, in schoolrooms and houses, and in cars or stores. Sometimes there is only a a little vapor, and sometimes there is a lot. Air that contains a lot of water vapor is moist, or humid. Weather forecasts often mention humid air or humidity.

No one can see water vapor in the air, for the molecules have no color and are very small. Yet you can easily make an experiment which shows that the vapor is there and is ready to become liquid again.

All you need is a drinking glass (or tumbler), some water, and some ice. Put the water and ice into the glass and watch it. Even when the air seems dry, tiny droplets soon cover the glass. On humid days the droplets grow into drops which often trickle down the sides of the tumbler.

Where does this liquid come from? Not from ice water in the tumbler, for water cannot soak through glass. The droplets come from water vapor that turns into liquid because your cold glass chills the air around it. Cool air cannot hold much vapor, since molecules do not bounce as fast as they do in air that is warm. As the molecules stop bouncing so fast, they settle down and form the droplets that cover your glass.

Air that goes up the sides of these mountains cools and its moisture forms clouds.

Clouds of Various Kinds

When moist air is cooled out of doors, water molecules cannot settle on glass. Instead, most of them collect on dust and other particles in the air. As more and more molecules cover the dust grains, they form droplets of water. When billions of droplets float near each other, they make up a cloud. Other clouds consist of ice. They form high up in the air, where it is so cold that droplets of water freeze.

Clouds develop almost everywhere, but the best place to see them do so is on high mountains surrounded by broad valleys or plains. Air that comes to these mountains contains water vapor, and it has to go up their slopes. As it does so, the vapor comes out of the air, making billions of tiny droplets. They soon form clouds that look like castles, ships with sails, or balls of bright, fluffy cotton.

These clouds are not cotton, of course, and they really are not bright. They look bright to us because the sun shines upon them, and they reflect its light. But mountain climbers who go into large clouds find them moist, chilly, and dark. Even when rain does not fall, water settles on trees, bushes, rocks, and the ground, making them dripping wet.

More than a hundred years ago, an English scientist named Luke Howard watched the clouds day after day. He found that there were several kinds, which came with different kinds of weather. Since most clouds had no English names, Luke Howard and other men gave them names made from ancient Latin words.

Cumulus (kewm′ yu luss) is one of those names; it means a "heap" or "pile." Cumulus clouds seem to be heaped into piles that are flat on the under side. Small ones are only 1,000 feet thick, but big ones measure a mile or more from their tops to their flattened bottoms.

Cumulus clouds often cover mountains, but they also form in other places on land or above the sea. They begin when warm air goes upward and cools, and they keep on growing as long as heat warms more air and makes it rise so high that its water vapor forms droplets. But when evening comes this process stops, and the clouds become small or disappear. Clear nights generally follow days when cumulus clouds sail through the sky.

Fracto-cumulus clouds. These are made by a strong wind, which is tearing cumulus clouds to pieces.

Strong winds often tear fluffy clouds into pieces. We call these pieces *fracto-cumulus* (frak′ toe-kewm′ yu luss), from the Latin word for "broken." They often rush across the sky as fast as automobiles can run on country roads. This helps us tell broken clouds from young ones that have not "grown up."

Strato-cumulus (stray′ toe-kewm′ yu luss) clouds are not so fluffy as cumulus clouds, and they spread out in irregular patches or layers. These clouds are common before and after thunderstorms. They also form at sunset, when cumulus clouds run together before they disappear.

The under side of strato-cumulus clouds that cover the sky. STANDARD OIL COMPANY (N.J.)

A *stratus* cloud (stray′ tuss) is a layer of water droplets that is always flat on top as well as on its under surface. As it comes toward us, its edge looks almost straight, with no thick parts and no thin ones. It may bring a light drizzle, but it almost never brings rain.

Some stratus clouds are small, but others cover hundreds of square miles. Most of them are less than 2,000 feet above the earth's surface, and many are only a few hundred feet. The biggest ones are as much as 1,000 feet thick, but thin ones measure only 50 feet from top to bottom. Hazy sunlight comes through these thin layers.

Stratus clouds often form near the ground at night and are not very thick. When such clouds hide the sky in the morning, they probably mean clear, warm weather later in the day.

"High fogs" are stratus clouds that begin about 900 feet above the surface and grow downward. This means that the under side of a "high fog" comes closer and closer to the ground as the cloud grows thick. Clouds of this kind are common near seacoasts, especially in California.

Cirrus clouds are made of ice and are very thin.

A thin layer of cirro-stratus clouds, with cirrus near the center. STANDARD OIL COMPANY (N.J.)

Nimbo-stratus (nim' bo-stray' tus) is Latin for "layer rain cloud." Nimbo-stratus clouds form thick layers that have no special shape. They look gray because they cut off a lot of sunlight, and they often cover the sky for many miles. Wisps of cloud that form on their under sides and hang down like torn rags are called *scud*.

Most nimbo-stratus clouds are 3,000 feet overhead, but some are only 100

51

feet and others are almost a mile. Their lower parts contain droplets, but the tops of big ones consist of icy flakes. Three fourths of these clouds bring rain or snow four or five hours after they appear. Some storms last longer than others, but many that come in the winter last about eight hours.

Cirrus (sirr′ us) means "curl," and clouds of this kind look like thin wisps or curls of white hair. Some are blown out straight, with a curve at one end,

Alto-cumulus clouds resemble cirro-cumulus, but are larger, thicker and lower.

but others form silvery nets that almost cover the sky. Those that stretch out in streaked and wispy bands are often called mare's tails.

Cirrus clouds form 5 to 7 miles above the ground, where the air is very cold. It freezes moisture into tiny needles of ice that float as easily as droplets. These needles sometimes form at night but disappear when morning sunshine turns them into vapor again.

Cirrus clouds that come before rain or snow are followed by *cirro-stratus* clouds, which also are made of ice. Most of them look like white veils, but some have milky patches and streaks. Both the sun and moon shine through them, making rings of hazy light called *halos*. These clouds may go as high as the highest cirrus, but the largest, thickest ones are no more than 3 ½ miles above the surface.

Alto-stratus (al' toe-stray' tus) clouds come after cirro-stratus when a storm is on the way. They look like dull blue or gray haze, with thick streaks or patches. Alto-stratus clouds either hide the sun and moon or let them show as spots of light that have no special shape.

These clouds are 2 to 3 ½ miles high. Their lower parts are made of water droplets, but their tops may contain needles of ice. They often bring snow-storms in winter, but heavy rains are not common. When conditions are right, rain falls steadily, but not very hard.

As you can guess from their name, *cirro-cumulus* clouds are about halfway between cirrus wisps and cumulus. They are so thin that sunlight shines through them, which means that they do not make shadows. Since they form at heights of 3 ½ to 5 miles, they are made of ice, not water.

This huge cumulo-nimbus cloud has a "veil" of icy cirrus at the top.

Cirro-cumulus clouds are often called mackerel skies, since they float overhead in flaky rows which look like markings on the fish called mackerel. These clouds are always seen near cirrus wisps or cirro-stratus veils. Like cirrus clouds, they often show best in the morning, before their grains and needles of ice evaporate.

Alto-cumulus clouds may float as much as 4 miles up in the sky, though many are only 6,000 feet. Air currents that rise and fall divide them into flakes or strips that often resemble mackerel skies. The under side of these clouds often looks gray, and the larger ones cast shadows. They generally contain

54

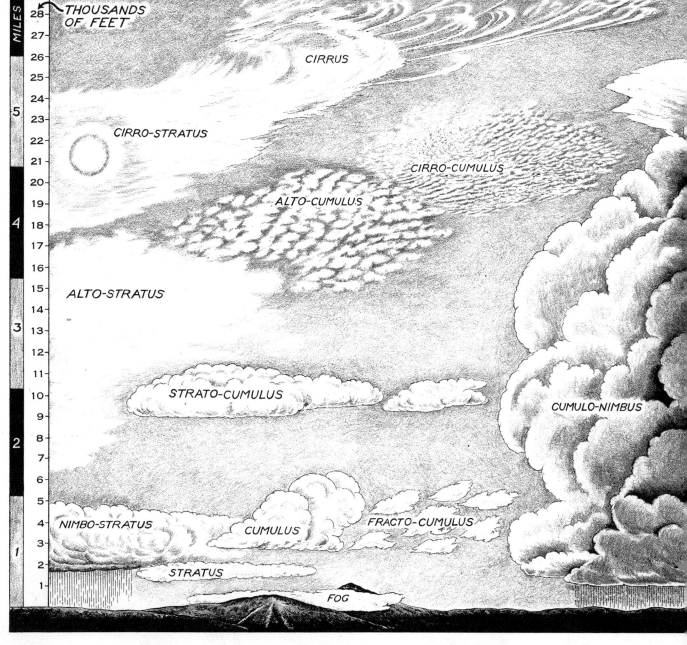

The most important kinds of clouds and the heights at which we generally see them.

droplets of water, though some are partly ice. When alto-cumulus clouds look like towers and castles, they mean that showers probably are coming in about eight hours.

Cumulo-nimbus is Latin for "piled-up rain clouds." All clouds of this kind are piled very high, and they often bring hail as well as rain. Since they cause thunder and lightning, too, we call them "thunderheads" even when they do not bring storms.

Thunderheads start out as fluffy cumulus clouds, about 2,000 feet above the ground. They generally form on moist summer days, and grow till they look like huge heads of cauliflower that are 5, 6 or even 7 miles high. Their tops become so cold that droplets of water freeze into ice and are blown out in sheets or wisps of cirrus.

When thunderheads are far away, they look gleaming white. As they come close they cut off the light and look dark blue, purple, or even greenish. Soon rain falls and lightning flashes, causing the crashes of thunder that give these clouds their name.

We shall find out more about storms from thunderheads on pages 63 to 67. Right now, let's look at the pictures of clouds again, to make sure we can name, or identify, real clouds as they come and go in the sky.

Haze, Fogs, and Rain

Have you ever wondered why faraway buildings often seem hazy? And why do hills often look blue, as if they were covered with smoke?

There are two answers to these questions. Sometimes the air really is filled with smoke from houses and factories, or from forest fires that are many miles away. But haze also may be caused by dust, by salt blown from ocean spray, or by tiny particles of water. All these things reflect light waves, sending them in every direction. This makes mountains, buildings, and trees look blue when we see them from far away.

Fogs are clouds that form near the earth's surface. Fog droplets are at least twenty times larger than haze droplets. They absorb so much light that foggy days often become as dark as evenings.

Evening fogs develop when air near the ground becomes so cool that its moisture turns into droplets. Valley fogs also form in the evening or at night, among hills and mountains. When morning comes these fogs "lift," or "burn up." This means that some of the sun's rays go through them, producing heat that warms the air and makes droplets evaporate. Currents of warm air rise, too, dividing the fog into patches that soon evaporate.

Many sea fogs form when moist, warm air blows over chilly water. Such fogs often become so thick that they look like smoke. When winds blow them to land they cover roads and cities and "reduce visibility to zero," which means that they keep everything from being seen. Many automobile accidents happen because drivers don't know what to do in these thick fogs.

Smog is fog of any kind mixed with smoke and gases. Smog generally forms when fog covers cities that have many factories. If gases in the smog are harmful, they often make people ill.

Wind is blowing a fog from the sea to the land. The sky above the fog is almost covered by strato-cumulus clouds.

Here a fog in the form of stratus clouds is creeping up valleys and over mountains under a stormy sky.

When fog drifts in a gentle breeze, droplets often bump into each other. Each time droplets bump, they stay together. In this way they grow larger and larger, until we call them *drizzle*, not fog.

Droplets of drizzle sprinkle down, but raindrops actually fall. They do because they are too big to stay up in the air. Small ones are ten times as large as drizzle droplets, and some are as big as this capital O.

Rain always falls from clouds, but the drops form in different ways in different parts of the world. In the hot Tropics, droplets fall and grow by capturing still more droplets. At last they become so large that they pelt down on the earth.

In cool, or temperate, parts of the world, raindrops begin as grains of ice that freeze near the tops of clouds. The ice grains fall and become larger as molecules and droplets of water freeze upon their surfaces. In time some grains become balls, but others grow into needles or snowflakes.

Have you ever watched snowflakes just as a storm begins? Many fall for a while and then rise as air currents whirl them upward. Some flakes go down and up several times before they come to the ground.

Ice and snow in clouds go up and down, too, just as snowflakes do near the ground. In each trip the particles grow larger, until they become so heavy that they cannot whirl upward again. Instead, they go down so far that they melt into raindrops and fall to the ground.

Ice storms are caused by rain that falls upon very cold land. The rain freezes into ice on pavements, sidewalks and snowbanks, and the sides of houses. Ice covers trees and bushes, too, and freezes around electric wires.

Rain falling from a small thunderhead.

Though the ice is very beautiful, it causes accidents, snaps wires and poles, and breaks many branches from trees.

When rains end, billions of tiny drops often stay in the air. When the sun shines on these drops, they divide the white sunlight into different colors. These colors appear in a curve which we call a rainbow. The lowest strip of color in each "bow" is purple, or violet. Then come two kinds of blue, followed by green, yellow, orange, and red. Sometimes a second bow shows above the first one. This second bow begins with red, but it generally stops with green or light blue and has no dark blue or purple strip.

Rain generally falls without any help from human beings. But sometimes this does not happen, and we have a dry spell, or drought.

For thousands of years people have tried to make rain fall during droughts. Old-time rainmakers blew horns, beat drums, shot cannons at the sky, or "made magic." Modern rainmakers look for clouds that are growing very fast and are cool at the top. Then they "seed" the clouds with chemicals that produce ice crystals, so that rain can fall.

Several chemicals are used, and some of them do bring rain from some clouds. Other clouds float away or disappear, without a drop of rain. Weather men are trying to find out why this happens. So long as no one really knows, rainmakers cannot promise to make rain during droughts.

Thunderstorms and Lightning

Hot, damp summer days often bring thunderstorms. The sky grows dark, lightning flashes, and thunder "claps" or rumbles. Rain and sometimes hail pelt down from cumulo-nimbus, or thunderhead, clouds.

Several things happen at once in a big thunderhead. At its front, hot air rushes upward so fast and so high that its moisture is frozen into ice grains. They fall and are carried upward again, growing larger as they go. At last they become so big and fall so far that they melt into raindrops.

The rain soon comes down so fast that we cannot see separate drops. It also begins to "drive," which means that it is blown by cool air that comes down from the cloud. This air blows in the direction toward which the storm is moving and so drives the raindrops down at a slant.

If the day has been very hot, hailstones as well as rain may come from a thunderhead. Hailstones form when grains of ice fall through the cloud and then are carried upward again. As they fall, they bump into raindrops and snowflakes. When they rise, these things freeze into a coating of ice. This happens over and over again, making hailstones as large as marbles, or even as big as eggs. One hailstone, which contained many frozen layers, was more than 5 inches thick and weighed 1½ pounds!

No one likes storms that bring hail, for the icy "stones" break glass in windows, greenhouses, and even in automobiles. Hailstones also knock fruit

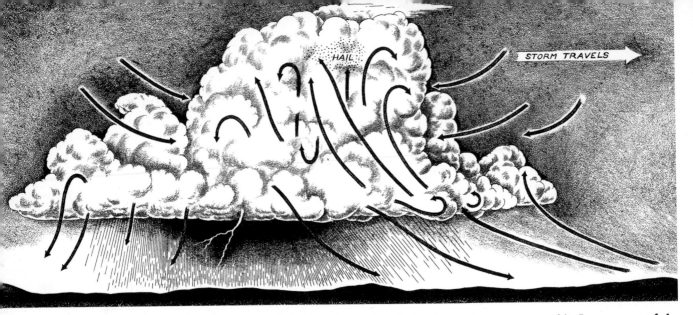

This picture shows how currents of air blow into a thunderhead and also come out of it. In one part of the cloud snow, water, and ice are forming hailstones.

and leaves from trees and damage crop plants growing in fields. In a few minutes, one hard hailstorm may destroy a farmer's crops for a year.

Only a few thunderheads bring hail, but almost all these big clouds cause lightning. Lightning is followed by thunder, which crashes and rumbles during a storm.

Lightning flashes because drops of water in the thunderhead contain two kinds of electrical charges, called positive and negative. Air currents tear many drops to pieces and pull off tiny bits called electrons, which contain the negative charges. The part of each drop that is left contains positive electricity.

This happens millions and billions of times as the thunderhead moves along. Air also carries the positive and negative charges to different parts of the cloud. When the charges become strong enough, they break through the air that divides them. Electrons rush back to the positively charged drops, heating and charging the air as they go. The charged air glows so brightly that it makes a flash of lightning.

This is the simplest kind of lightning — the kind that goes from one part of the cloud to another. Lightning that goes from the cloud to the ground is not so simple, but this is how it seems to form.

Hailstones showing layers formed as they went up and down in a cloud.

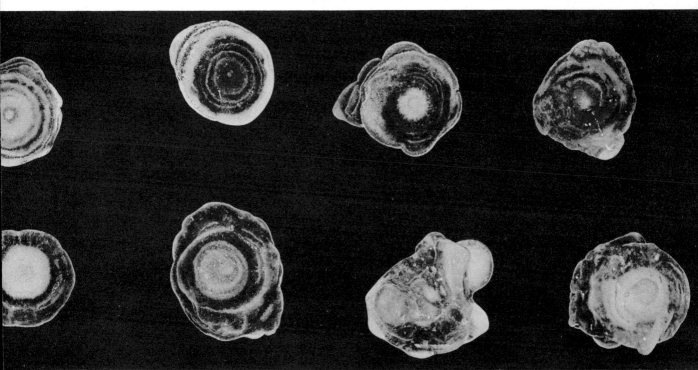

A strong charge in a thunderhead makes a charge of the opposite kind develop at the surface of the ground. Soon electrons start to move toward the ground, making a path called a "streamer," which may be single or may divide. More electrons complete the streamer, and then a huge swarm travel along it. They, too, heat the air, causing the lightning flash.

We often speak of "chain" lightning and "heat" lightning as if they

"Chain" lightning from a thunderstorm. The trees are one half mile away, but some of the lightning is closer.
U.S. WEATHER BUREAU—WALBROOK.

were different kinds. Actually, chain lightning is the bright, nearby flashes which we can see clearly. Some heat lightning consists of flashes that glow dimly because they are inside large clouds. Other heat lightning is flashes that are far away. Instead of seeing the lightning itself, we see its light reflected from the surfaces of clouds.

As electrons shoot through the air, making it glow, they do something else. They make the air so hot that it explodes, causing the noise which we call thunder. Thunder produced by nearby lightning makes a sharp crash, or "clap." Thunder that booms and rumbles is so far away that we hear its sound echo from clouds and from high hills or mountains.

Light travels so fast that we see lightning almost as soon as it flashes, but sound takes five seconds to travel a mile. When you see lightning that seems to be far away, count the number of seconds until you hear the sound of thunder. If you don't have a watch, say "One lollipop, two lollipops," and so on. If you count to ten seconds (or ten lollipops), the lightning was 2 miles away. How far away is a flash of lightning if you wait three seconds before you hear thunder?

Snowflakes and Snowstorms

Most rains that fall outside the Tropics begin as ice or snow that forms high up in clouds. If the snow melts, it becomes raindrops. If it does not melt, it comes to the ground in the form of snowflakes. Instead of causing rain, the flakes make a snowstorm.

Shall we watch a rain that turns into a snowstorm? It begins on a winter day when clouds of the kind called nimbo-stratus seem to be everywhere. Their dark gray color tells us that they are thick. Their name, as we already know, means a "rainy layer."

The nimbo-stratus clouds fit their name, for rain soon begins to fall. Then the rain stops and snowflakes come down. They tell us that the lower part of the clouds has grown cold, and so has the air below them. They are much too cold to melt snowflakes and turn them into rain.

We can see snowflakes plainly as they come through the air. But we can see them still better if we let them fall on something that is black and colder than freezing, so they will not melt.

We look at some of these fallen snowflakes through a magnifying glass. Most of them have six sides or points, showing that they are ice crystals. Some also have many side branches which make them look like tiny white ferns. Flakes that seem to be very large really are tangles of crystals. Their branches caught and held them together as they came down to the ground.

Snowflakes at the left formed high in the air, two in the center formed lower down, and those at the right began high up but got their points in the lower part of a cloud.

Some weather men study snow crystals in order to find out how they are made. Though no one has learned for certain, here is what these weather men think:

Snow crystals that are solid, with three or six sides, probably form at the tops of clouds, where the air does not contain much moisture. These flakes seem to grow so slowly that they have time to become solid. They are often the first and the last ones to fall during a widespread storm.

Snowflakes with six points and many branches probably form lower down in clouds, where there is much more moisture and the air is not so cold. This means that crystals take shape and grow rapidly.

Other snowflakes are called *composite* (kom poz' it), which means that they are made up of more than one type. Such flakes probably begin high up in the air, where they become small and solid. Then they fall to the lower

This moist snow clings to trees and bushes, and forms a fluffy layer on the ground. When it melts it will become moisture that can sink into the soil.

part of the clouds, where there is lots of moisture. There the flakes quickly develop points and branches. Soon they start to fall again, and go all the way to the ground.

We know that snow falls upon places where the winter weather grows cold. Snow also falls upon high, cold mountains at almost any time of the year. Snowstorms often whirl around mountain tops in July and August, while rain falls on lower slopes and in valleys.

Snowstorms are not always cold, even though they come in winter. Watch closely when snowflakes fall on a day that is not very cool. The first flakes quickly melt, but others keep on falling. They cling to roofs and branches, which often bend down under their weight, and they form a moist white layer on the ground. This moist snow is fine for making snowmen, snowballs, and snowhouses or forts.

Cold, "dry" snowflakes do not cling to trees and branches, and they do not pack together in snowballs. They often fall rapidly or are driven along by the wind. When this happens, the snow is piled up in drifts that become several feet deep.

We often think of a blizzard as a bad snowstorm. Actually, it is a combination of very strong wind, very cold weather, and dry, "powdery" snow. The wind blows the powdery snow from the ground and mixes it with flakes that come down from the clouds. The blowing snow hides buildings and fences, and piles up in drifts that block highways and railroads. Both people and animals get lost, and the cold wind often freezes them before they can find shelter.

Although blizzards do a great deal of harm, ordinary wet snows are useful. They pile moisture upon the ground, where it can melt slowly and sink into the soil. There the moisture is ready for use by plants that will grow in the spring.

Loose snow also makes a fluffy blanket which covers low plants and the ground. This blanket prevents very cold air from reaching the ground, and it keeps the soil from losing too much heat. Many plants that would freeze if the ground were bare can live safely under snow.

Animals and even people also use snow to keep themselves warm. Wild mice often hide under snowbanks and gophers dig tunnels in them when they hunt for food. Bears often sleep all winter under logs that are covered by snowdrifts. In the North, where winter lasts for months, Eskimos cut snow into blocks and use them to build houses. In these snowhouses the people keep warm at night and on days when terrible storms blow over the snowy land.

Dew and Frost

We sometimes say that dew "falls," as if it came down from clouds, like rain. Actually, most dew forms where we find it, on bushes, grass, spider webs, and weeds. It is made from water vapor in moist air that is near the ground.

When we go outdoors on a clear summer night we notice that rocks and plants grow cool as they lose heat made from the sun's rays during the daytime. At last they become so chilly that they turn water vapor into droplets when it touches them. When the droplets run together they form dewdrops that glitter brightly when the sun comes up.

Can you guess why dew forms on clear nights, but not when the sky is cloudy? It does so because thick clouds act like a blanket that keeps rocks, grass, and other plants from cooling rapidly. They remain so warm that they cannot chill water vapor and turn it into dew. We also see no dew in very dry weather, for the air does not contain enough moisture to make drops on plants or the ground.

———

If you live where the winter weather grows cold, you are sure to see frost on windows. It may cover the glass with a smooth white coat. It also may form beautiful patterns which look like lace, flowers, or ferns.

This frost is made up of small, thin crystals of ice, and it is formed by water vapor in the air that fills your home. When vapor touches cold win-

73

dows, it freezes and turns into frost. This happens most often at night, when stoves and furnaces generally send out less heat than they do in the daytime, and when sunlight does not warm windows.

The ice crystals that make up frost form like those in snowflakes. Since frost crystals are fastened to glass, however, they cannot grow into perfect six-sided flakes or crystals with delicate points. They often get into each

Dewdrops on a spider web glisten as the sun shines upon them.

At the left are frost patterns on a window pane. At the right, crystals and flakes of hoar frost cover part of a grape vine.

other's way, and they cluster around scratches and bits of dirt. You can see four long scratches in the frost shown on page 75.

Frost also forms outdoors, especially in the autumn and spring. During these seasons the days may be warm and sunny, but things cool off rapidly at night. Grass, weeds, and bushes grow cold, and so do many roofs and trees. Water vapor that touches them is frozen. When morning comes, we find them coated with crystals of ice.

Hoar frost is a thick, flaky type that forms when air which contains a great deal of water vapor suddenly comes against things that are very cold. The vapor freezes into thin, flat crystals of ice. They often form on top of each other, covering twigs and branches with a thick white coat.

Hoar frost is beautiful, but it does not last very long. Sunshine quickly melts the crystals, and breezes make them fall. If a hoar frost forms near your home, eat an early breakfast and go outdoors to see it. Even then, you may find that many crystals have fallen from the trees.

———————

Most common frost forms near the ground, but it also covers the wings of airplanes that get cold and then fly through moist air. A coat of crystals makes the planes heavy, but it is not dangerous, like rime or clear ice.

The rime that covers airplanes forms when cold planes fly into thin clouds made of very small droplets. The droplets freeze into grainy ice that is many times heavier than frost. It weighs so much that the planes sometimes "stall" and have to make emergency landings.

Clear ice is most likely to form in mists, light rains, and clouds that contain a great deal of water but are not much colder than freezing. When a cold plane flies into one of these clouds, "supercooled" droplets freeze on the wings, making a coat of ice that grows thicker every second. If de-icers cannot break this ice off, it makes the plane lose altitude or even plunge to the ground.

Where Weather Comes From

"Showers tomorrow morning," the weather man may say. "Skies will clear and wind will blow in the afternoon."

In winter the forecasts tell of cold weather, but in spring they say that days will grow warmer. In the summer the forecasts predict heat waves, thunderstorms, or long dry spells when there will be no rain. Where do all these kinds of weather come from? And how can the weather man tell which kind we shall have tomorrow or next week?

To find the answers to these questions, we take another trip in our imaginary space ship. We also use the spyglass that lets us see air as well as water and land.

The first thing we notice as we look at the earth is several big *source regions*. These are places where the air moves slowly or almost stands still for days or even weeks at a time. As the air stays in these regions, it is changed by its surroundings. The Gulf of Mexcio, for example, makes air masses warm and humid, but air that stays over northern Canada and Alaska becomes dry and cold.

Air that is changed in a source region is known as an air mass. Our imaginary spyglass makes an air mass look like a huge flattened cloud that is hundreds of miles wide and several miles in thickness. Actually, of course, the cloud is air and cannot be seen.

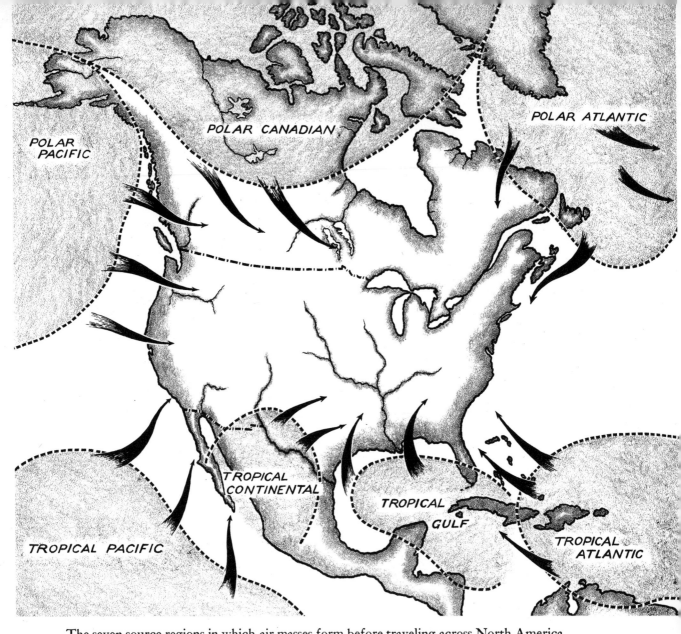

The seven source regions in which air masses form before traveling across North America.

After staying in one place for a while, air masses drift away and begin to travel. Air masses that make weather in North America come from seven principal regions, which are shown on page 78.

Polar Canadian air masses form in the North, between Alaska and Greenland. Most of them then travel southeastward across Canada and the northern part of the United States. They bring cool, dry weather in summer, but when winter comes they turn cold. Our worst "cold snaps" are caused by Polar Canadian air that travels southeastward in the wintertime.

Polar Pacific air masses come from the northern Pacific Ocean and southwestern Alaska. These air masses are cool but not very cold, and they contain a great deal of moisture. They travel to the Pacific coast, where their moisture turns into clouds that send down rain or snow as they are carried over high mountains.

Polar Atlantic air masses begin over the northern Atlantic Ocean. Most of them travel toward Europe, but a few drift to the shores of Canada and the United States. In the summer they are cool and moist and bring fogs or low stratus clouds, but in winter they cause heavy snow.

Tropical Continental air masses form over Mexico and the Southwest during summer months. They are hot and dry, and they generally bring clear skies as they travel northeastward across the United States.

Tropical Gulf and Tropical Atlantic air masses are very much alike. They form over warm seas and flow northward to the United States. When they get there they turn and drift northeastward. Tropical Atlantic masses stay near the coast, but masses from the Gulf of Mexico go inland. They

Air from the Gulf of Mexico contains a great deal of moisture. Here we see a thunderhead and alto-stratus clouds in a humid Tropical Gulf air mass.

STANDARD OIL COMPANY, (N.J.)

often travel from Texas to Canada or eastward to the Atlantic Ocean. These tropical air masses are hot in summer and are mild or warm in the winter. During July and August they cause humid heat waves with thunderstorms and sometimes with tornadoes. In the autumn and winter these moist air masses often produce fogs, rains, and snowstorms.

Tropical Pacific air masses form above warm parts of the Pacific Ocean. These air masses also are warm and humid, but they never are quite so moist as air from the Gulf of Mexico. Tropical Pacific air masses cause stratus clouds near the Pacific coast and often send down rain or snow as they cross mountain ranges.

Well, these are the answers to our questions. Our weather is produced by huge masses of air that come from different source regions and travel in different ways across North America. The weather man finds out what each air mass is like when it starts out, and how it is going to cross our country. He also finds out how fast it is traveling. When he puts all these facts together, he can tell what kind of air is coming and when it will arrive.

MOIST, CLEAR AIR FROM THE SEA

GROWS CLOUDY AS IT CLIMBS MOUNTAINS

An air mass changes as it climbs high mountains, becoming cool and cloudy.

How Air Masses Change

Air masses bring different kinds of weather as they come from different source regions. The masses also change and make still more kinds of weather as they travel over the land.

On this page, for example, we see a mass of warm, moist air that starts eastward from the Pacific Ocean. At first the air is clear, but it cools and becomes cloudy as it climbs the mountains. On page 83 the clouds reach the mountain tops, where they become so cold that their water falls as rain or snow. This makes the air mass dry — so dry that no moisture is left to fall on level land east of the mountains.

Other changes take place when tropical air from the Gulf of Mexico crosses the central United States in July or August. The air is warm as well as moist when it comes from the sea, but the hot land makes it still warmer. Convection currents soon begin to rise, carrying the humid air so high that

RAIN OR SNOW FALLS ON THE MOUNTAINS

THE AIR IS DRY WHEN IT COMES TO THE PLAINS

The same air becomes rainy and then dries out as it goes over the mountains and comes down to low plains.

its moisture forms thunderheads, or cumulo-nimbus clouds. Hard rains often fall from such clouds, and sometimes are followed by hail. Though each storm may be small and may last only a few minutes, hundreds of storms may develop before the air mass finally disappears over the Atlantic Ocean.

Different changes take place when a Tropical Gulf air mass travels northeastward in winter. This air also is warm and moist, but the ground is now cold instead of hot. At first the cold land chills the air, turning moisture near the ground into fog or drizzle. Then, as the mass keeps on going, it begins to creep upward over air that is cold. This makes clouds that become larger and thicker, like those shown ahead of the warm front on page 89. Their moisture becomes chilly rain and then turns into snow.

Dry air masses change as much as air that is moist and warm. Suppose that a Polar Canadian mass comes down from the North just as winter begins. At first the air is cold and dry, but it warms up a little as it blows over land that has not been covered with snow. The air grows still warmer over the Great Lakes, where it also gets water vapor that turns into clouds. Land soon cools the air again and its clouds become snow that falls on the Appalachian Mountains. After that, the air starts downhill and begins to warm up. It is dry and is not very cold when it flows over low land beside the Atlantic Ocean.

If air masses change a great deal, they may bring weather that does not fit the forecasts. Moist air, for example, may turn so cold that it brings snow instead of rain. Cold Canadian air also may cross the Great Lakes so fast that it does not become humid. When this happens the cold air mass brings clear weather, even though forecasts may have said it would bring rain or snow.

A warm air mass grows cold as it travels northeastward in the winter, but cold air that travels southeastward grows warmer and becomes humid.

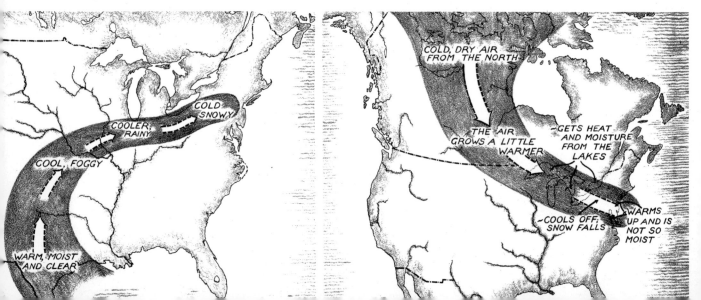

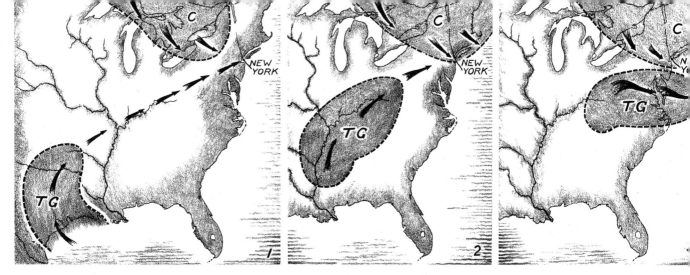

Here warm, moist air (TG) from the Gulf of Mexico is turned aside by a cold air mass (C) that almost stops moving. This means that weather in New York and the region south of it will not fit forecasts made while the moist air was traveling northeastward.

Forecasts also are wrong when air masses don't go where they are supposed to. In the first map on page 85, for example, moist air (TG) that has come from the Gulf of Mexico is beginning to travel toward New York. It should get there after the dry, cold air mass (C) has passed, and should cause mild weather and rain.

Map 2 shows the moist air going toward New York, but the cold air is moving so slowly that it will not get out of the way. In Map 3, the moist air does just what you have to do when people stand where you want to go. You turn aside, and so does the TG air mass. It brings mild weather and rain to places as far south as North Carolina, but does not affect New York's weather, which remains clear and cold.

You may not want to remember these things, and you do not need to, for weather maps will tell you about them. But you will want to remember that air masses change day after day as they travel across our continent. Some of these changes can be predicted, but others take place when no one expects them. So do changes in the speed of air masses and the directions in which they travel. When these unpredictable things happen, weather men make forecasts that turn out to be wrong.

What Happens on Fronts

Let's get into our imaginary space ship again and sail away to a place where we can watch the air masses that cross North America. We see them change as they go over mountains, lakes, and deserts, or over places that are covered with snow when winter comes.

We notice other things, too — things that are very important. Although most air masses travel eastward across southern Canada and the United States, they don't travel alone and in one direction, at speeds that are always the same. Air masses come from different directions at once, and they travel at different speeds. During summer, the average speed is about 20 miles per hour, or 480 to 500 miles per day. In winter, the speed goes up to about 700 miles a day. But warm masses may travel only 10 miles per hour, though some go 20 or 25. Some cold masses travel faster than that, but others (like the one on page 85) go so slowly that they almost stand still.

You know what happens when a crowd of people walk in different directions and at different speeds. They jostle, push and bump into each other, and sometimes cause a lot of excitement.

Air masses that go in different directions also jostle and push, and they do exciting things to the weather. They make winds blow one way and then another, and they send temperatures up or down. They also cause clouds, long rains, and snows that fall when the weather is too cold for rain.

Thunderstorms often come along a cold front, where cool air pushes against air that is warm and humid. But the storms will stop soon after the cold front moves on.

Most of these exciting things happen where two different air masses come together. Instead of mixing, they produce a break which weather men call a "surface of discontinuity." Where this surface comes down to the sea, a big lake, or the land, it becomes a *front*. Fronts are the boundary lines between different air masses which we often see on weather maps.

Fronts are either warm or cold. A cold front is the boundary line where an oncoming mass of cold air pushes against air that is warm. A warm front is the boundary where a warm air mass catches up with a cold mass that is ahead of it.

Suppose we now go back to the ground and see what happens as a cool air mass travels toward the east, pushing against air that is warm.

Long before the cool air arrives, it begins to force the warm air upward. This causes gray alto-cumulus clouds, and then cumulus clouds appear. As

Here we see how clouds and the weather change as a warm front approaches. Since the warm air is humid, rain may last for a long time.

the cold front comes near, the warm air goes higher and its moisture makes huge cumulo-nimbus clouds that are 4, 5, or even 7 miles high. Rain falls from them in the summer, but when winter comes they send snow.

While rain is falling from thunderheads, the cold front arrives. The wind whips to and fro and then changes, so that it blows from the west or northwest. The air becomes cooler, too. Temperatures sometimes drop five or even ten degrees in fifteen or twenty minutes.

Rain or snow may not stop so quickly, for thick nimbo-stratus clouds often form behind the thunderheads and above the advancing cold air. Rain or snow also may fall from flat-looking strato-cumulus clouds that float behind the cold front. But when these clouds are blown away, the sky becomes clear. We have bright, cool, dry weather, which is just the kind we expect from a cool, dry air mass.

Since warm air masses do not travel so fast as cold ones, they cannot cause such sudden changes. In spite of this they give better warnings of stormy weather to come.

We know that warm air weighs less than cool air. This means that warm air can't push cool air upward or hustle it out of the way. In fact, cool air generally gets out of the way so slowly that warm air flows over it, just as

Cirrus clouds are turning into a cirro-stratus and then thick alto-stratus as a warm front moves eastward. Rain will fall when the alto-stratus clouds are followed by nimbo-stratus.

waves from a lake or the ocean flow over a beach. When a warm air mass overtakes a cool one, the warm air flows up a slope that starts at the sea or the ground and goes to a height of 4 or 5 miles. Since this slope is not so steep as most beaches, it may be 500 miles in width. Warm air may travel overhead for a day or two, coming lower and lower until the warm front actually arrives.

Our first hint of a warm front comes when we see thin cirrus clouds about 5 miles up in the air. But this is only a hint, for cirrus clouds sometimes form over cool, dry air masses. When that happens, the icy clouds go as high as 7 miles, but they do not tell us much about the kind of weather that is coming.

We know that a warm front is above us when the clouds go lower and lower and become cirro-stratus sheets that thicken until they look dull or gray. Several hours may go by before this happens, and the sky becomes hazy white. These clouds are about 4 miles above the surface of the earth.

As the warm air keeps on moving, it comes lower and lower. The clouds become lower and thicker, too. They form alto-stratus sheets and then nimbo-stratus masses that bring rain or snow. The under side of these dark storm clouds may be only 1,000 feet above our heads.

When nimbo-stratus clouds disappear, we know that the warm front has passed. In summertime the rain stops, the sky clears slowly, and the weather becomes mild and moist. But when land or sea is cold, the warm air mass is cooled and its moisture forms stratus or strato-cumulus clouds which are so low that we call them fog.

Storms That Whirl

On hot, dry summer days we often see "dust devils," or whirlwinds. They are winds that go round and round like corkscrews, rising as they whirl. They blow dirt and papers from city streets, or take dust and dead weeds from fields and country roads.

Many whirlwinds are only a few feet wide and 20 to 50 feet high, but on bare, hot deserts of the West they often become much larger. Some desert whirlwinds rise as much as 1,000 feet above the surface and travel a mile or more before they disappear.

Tornadoes are much larger than whirlwinds, though they also are made of air that whirls round and round. Many people call them "twisters," and others call them "cyclones." They are commonest in the states of Kansas, Missouri, and Iowa, but they may form almost anywhere east of the Rocky Mountains. They sometimes appear on southwestern deserts and even in valleys near the Pacific coast.

Tornadoes may blow on hot summer afternoons that also are very humid. But most of these storms come in the spring, when cold Polar Pacific air masses push warm, moist air out of the way. The first sign of a "twister" is tumbled clouds that form where winds blow from different directions. Then some of the cool air pushes into the moist air, which begins to rise. It produces a big cumulo-nimbus cloud, or thunderhead, that grows larger very rapidly. The

STORM TRAVELS

A tornado. Arrows show how air whirls into the storm and how winds blow inside the funnel.

cloud's color also changes from white to dark blue or bluish gray and then to greenish black.

Next the rising air begins to whirl in a direction opposite to the way in which a clock's hands turn. As the air whirls and rises it cools, and its moisture forms streamers of cloud that curve like the arms of a pinwheel. Faster and faster goes the air, while the streamers come closer and closer together. At last they form a hollow, funnel-shaped cloud under the big, billowy one. This funnel-shaped cloud, with the wind that makes it, is the "twister," or tornado.

Some tornadoes stay up in the sky, never coming down to earth. Others become long funnels that extend downward 2,000 or 3,000 feet, until they reach the ground. Their gray color and their shape make them look like an elephant's trunk.

A tornado that reaches the ground is terrible and dangerous. The whirling wind blows at speeds of 200 to 300 miles per hour and roars like dozens of jet airplanes. Lightning flashes inside the funnel, and small whirlwinds appear around it. The wind pulls up trees, breaks telephone poles, carries rubbish upward, and sometimes blows trains from railroad tracks. At the center of the storm, where the air rises, the pressure becomes very low. When the funnel goes over houses and barns, the much greater pressure of air inside them makes the buildings explode. Then the wind whirls boards and furniture into the air. It even picks up such heavy things as bathtubs or stoves and carries them away.

While the wind in a tornado whirls round and round, the whole storm travels toward the east or northeast. It goes at a speed of 20 to 60 miles per hour, twisting from side to side, changing shape, and sometimes rising high above the ground. In a half hour it may disappear, though a few huge tornadoes keep going for several hours. In that time they travel as much as 300 miles.

———————

Waterspouts are big whirlwinds or small tornadoes that form over large lakes or the sea. The whirling wind carries spray upward, while moisture in the rising air forms a dark funnel of cloud, and rain falls from the thunderhead above it. Most waterspouts are able to wreck small boats, and big spouts can damage large ships. One of the largest waterspouts ever seen developed and changed like a tornado, and was 3,600 feet high. Its funnel was 240 feet wide at the bottom and more than 800 feet wide at the top, where it joined the thunderhead.

———————

Hurricanes are whirling storms that form over tropical seas. They do not blow as fast as the winds in tornadoes, but the storms themselves are many times larger. They travel farther than tornadoes, too, and they do much more harm.

If we could sail many miles up in the air, we might watch hurricanes develop. At first each storm is only a region where hot, moist air begins to rise. Higher and higher it goes, while more air blows in to take its place. This air comes from all directions and soon begins to whirl. It turns "counterclockwise," which means that it goes just opposite to the hands of a clock.

As the moist air goes upward, thunderheads form and spread out in a huge pancake of clouds with a hole, or "eye," at the center. The air inside

At the left is a space-ship view of a hurricane southeast of Florida. Arrows on the map at the right show the paths hurricanes often take.

this eye is calm, but the winds that whirl around it blow at speeds of 80 to 150 miles per hour. The whole storm travels northward at a rate of 10 to 15 miles per hour.

While a hurricane is over the ocean, it stirs up huge waves and sends down hard rains. When the storm comes to land, it brings more rain and drives the waves onshore. They wreck boats and smash buildings, while wind breaks windows, blows houses to pieces, and bends trees so far that they break or are pulled up by the roots.

Most North American hurricanes come in the late summer or fall. Those on the Pacific Ocean travel northward near Mexico, but almost never reach the land. Hurricanes that come from the Atlantic Ocean and the Caribbean Sea often travel past Cuba and nearby islands till they come to the United

States. Some "die out" on the Gulf of Mexico or near Florida, but others keep on going till they reach Canada. Weather men watch these hurricanes and send out warnings that tell which way the storms are going and how fast they move.

Have you ever read about terrible storms called *baguios* (ba ghee′ oze) or typhoons? Baguios really are hurricanes that blow over the Philippine Islands, and typhoons are hurricanes of China and Japan. Australian hurricanes are known as willy-willies. Since willy-willies form on the southern half of the earth, their winds blow in the opposite direction from those in the northern hemisphere.

Cyclones, Lows, and Highs

Hurricanes are sometimes called cyclones, and so are tornadoes. But most cyclones are larger than these storms, and their winds do not blow so fast. They also are so common that they cause much of our weather.

Most of these large cyclones form where two different air masses meet and struggle against each other. In the maps on page 99, for example, a cool air mass is pushing against a warm one, and winds in the two masses blow in opposite directions. The cyclone begins in Map 2, when warm air bulges into the cool mass. At first the bulge is not very big, but it makes winds blow in curves instead of straight. The bulge also grows larger and larger, until it becomes a tongue of warm air (Map 3), with a warm front on one side and a cold front on the other.

As the tongue of warm air grows long and narrow, winds blow toward the tip. As you see from the arrows on Map 4, these winds come from all directions. They form a spiral that explains the name cyclone, which means "something that whirls round and round."

Let's now imagine we can watch a cyclone travel from the west toward the east across North America. From our space ship it looks like a huge pinwheel with patches of clouds in the arms. On the ground, our first sign that the cyclone is coming is given by wind that blows from the southeast, the east, or even from the northeast. Hours later, the warm front arrives, bringing

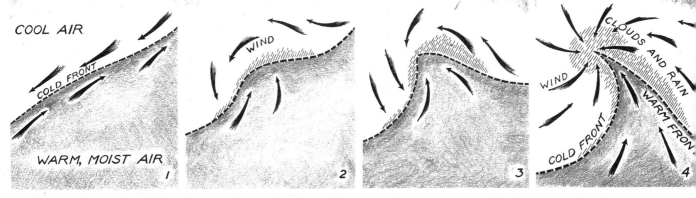

These four maps show how a cyclone forms as a warm air mass bulges farther and farther into one that is cool.

clouds that grow lower and thicker until they send down rain or snow. Next comes the tongue of warm, moist air, in which the weather is damp though it may be partly clear. Then the cold front arrives, causing more showers or snow. Last of all comes the cool air mass, which brings cool, clear weather and winds that blow from the west.

In many cyclones, the cold front moves faster than the warm front and finally catches up with it. That has happened in Map 5 on page 100, where cool air is pushing against cool air, and warm air in the cyclone has been forced high above the ground. Weather men call this an *occlusion* (oh kloo'-zhun), or an *occluded front*.

We can tell an occlusion by its clouds and the kinds of weather it brings. The clouds change from cirrus to nimbo-stratus and then to cumulus or even thunderheads. The weather goes from clear and cool to dark and stormy, and back to clear and cool again.

Cyclones help us understand two words that are often used in weather forecasts. They are *high* and *low*.

We know that cold air weighs more than warm air, and that dry air is heavier than air containing a lot of water vapor. But instead of telling how much air weighs, we tell how hard it presses against the sea or land. This air pressure is measured with a *barometer* (ba rom′ i ter).

Some barometers have springs and pointers much like those on scales. But the best barometers are long tubes of glass partly filled with mercury, or quicksilver, and open at one end. When the air is heavy, it pushes the mercury high up in the glass, but when the air is light it does not push the mercury so far. This explains why the weather man says that the barometer is rising

Map 5 shows how the cyclone on page 99 became an occlusion. In the picture we see what happens to weather as the occlusion goes past.

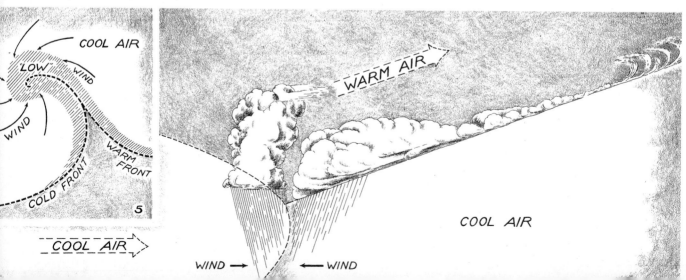

COOL, DRY AIR

WARM, MOIST AIR

COOL AIR

The black marks show how pressure varied in different parts of a cyclone, or low. Mercury in the barometers is lowest where the air is humid and highest where it is cool and dry.

or falling, or is steady. A rising barometer means that the air pressure is increasing, but a falling barometer means that it is becoming less. When the barometer is steady, the air pressure does not change.

There are two ways to measure pressure — in inches and in millibars. At sea level, on an ordinary clear day, air pushes the mercury in a barometer to a height of about 30 inches. We therefore say that the pressure is 30 inches. But on a warm, humid day, the pressure may be only 29.5 or 29 inches, and it may fall lower than that.

A millibar is a much smaller measure, and it does not need decimals. A pressure of 30.21 inches, for example, is 1,023 millibars, and 29.5 inches is 999 millibars.

If we could cut a slice through the center of a cyclone, we would find a sloping mass of cool air at each side and a tongue of warm, moist air in the middle. If a barometer is carried through the cyclone, the mercury will be high when we start but will "fall" lower and lower till we come to the center. After that, it begins to rise, which means that the pressure increases until we come to the other side of the cyclone.

A cyclone, then, is a place where the air pressure is low. We might call it a "low-pressure area," but *low* does just as well and is easier to say.

Most lows are round or oval. The everyday kind may be very large, too — more than 1,000 miles across. Hurricanes, or tropical cyclones, are smaller. Most of them are only 100 to 150 miles wide.

You can guess what *highs* are from their name. The "highest" highs are masses of cool, dry air, shaped like huge, irregular domes that are 6 or 7 miles thick. Pressure is highest at the center of each dome, and becomes lower toward the edges. This lets air blow away from the center, making strong winds when it blows into cyclones or toward warm, moist air masses. We often notice these winds when the weather turns dry after humid, rainy spells. Most high-pressure winds come from the west or northwest, and they often blow at night as well as in the daytime.

Reading the Weather Map

Many newspapers publish maps that show what the weather is and how it is changing. Some of these maps are specially drawn, but others are prepared by the United States Weather Bureau.

Three maps prepared by the Weather Bureau are shown on pages 104 and 106. On those maps we see the words LOW and HIGH, which we already know. We also see many lines that wind or zigzag across the land and sometimes go out to sea. Each line is called an *isobar* (eye' so bar), a name that means "equal pressure." Isobars connect places where the air pressure is the same. It is shown on the maps in numbers — small numbers that are read in inches and big ones that mean millibars. The numbers 30.03 and 1017, for example, mean air pressure that pushes the mercury in barometers to a height of 30 and 3 hundredths inches, or 1,017 millibars.

The edges of air masses, or fronts, are drawn on the map in heavy lines that often cross the isobars. Cold fronts have blunt black points that show which way the cool air is moving. Warm fronts are marked by half dots, also on the side toward which the air mass is going. Fronts that stand still, or are stationary, have half dots on one side and points on the other. Occluded fronts, which come in lows, have both points and half dots on one side.

Among the lines are wind "arrows," which end in round heads. A dot or circle without a line means that there is no wind. A line tells us that the air

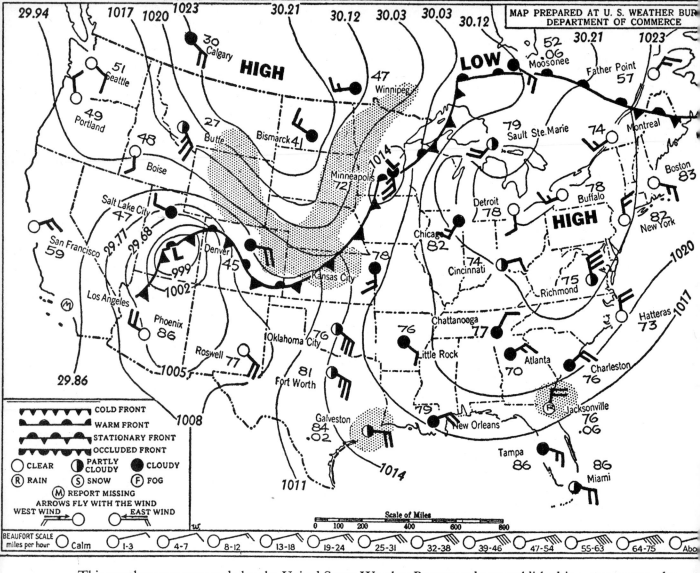

This weather map was made by the United States Weather Bureau and was published in a newspaper, the New York *Times*.

is moving, and short "tails" show how fast. Arrows also tell which way the wind is blowing — always toward the head. An empty arrowhead means clear weather, but a head that is half black tells us that these are clouds. A black head shows that clouds cover the sky, which is overcast. The letters R, S, and F mean rain, snow, and fog. Shading shows where rain or snow fell less than six hours before the map was made, and numbers with the names of places tell the temperature.

———————

Now that we know how to read weather maps, let's find out how to use them. We choose a day in June, when we are planning a picnic. The weather map shows that a high on the Atlantic coast is going out over the ocean. Farther west there is a trough of low pressure that extends from Canada to the Gulf of Mexico. There is another low in the Southwest, but a high covers the northwestern United States and nearby parts of Canada.

This map means different things, depending upon where we live. If our homes are near the Atlantic coast, we know that tomorrow and the next day will be cloudy or rainy, so we put off our picnic. But if we live anywhere between Detroit and San Francisco, we know that tomorrow probably will be sunny but rather cool for an outing. Day after tomorrow also will be fine in many places, though clouds will cover the sky from Minnesota to the Pacific coast. Sure enough — we find them marked on the map for June 4 when it is printed in the newspaper. We can look up and see the clouds themselves if we live in Minneapolis, Bismarck, Butte, or Seattle, or almost anywhere between those four cities.

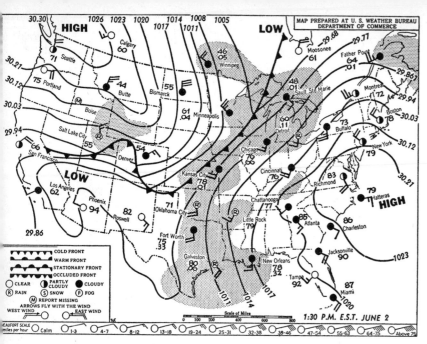

The map at the left shows weather in the United States and Canada on a day early in June. If you lived near the Atlantic coast, would you plan a picnic for the next day or the day after?

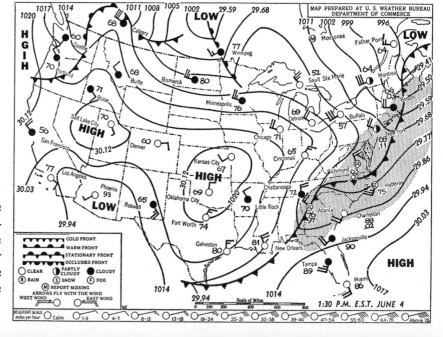

The map at the right shows how the weather has changed in two days. Although two big highs cover most of the United States, there are clouds in many regions. Both these maps, prepared by the Weather Bureau, were published in the New York *Times*.

This is what the weather might look like if we could see it from a space ship. The large white patches are made by clouds that cover the sky.

If we could sail far out into space, we would actually see the weather that is shown on maps. It would look a good deal like the picture on this page, which shows warm fronts, cold fronts, and a hurricane near Florida. Still, we can't see isobars, and clouds hide rains that may be falling. So a view from our make-believe space ship really does not show as much as we can learn from a map!

Making Our Own Forecasts

People often say that east winds bring snow or rain, but that west winds mean fair weather. Is that really true? And do other signs tell us what tomorrow's weather will be?

We can easily answer the first of these questions. Everyday winds almost never *bring* snow or rain, which are made from moisture that comes in huge masses of air. Though air masses travel in various directions, most of them go toward the east. So do the fronts between air masses, and the lows in which rain and snow often fall.

Still, east winds often mean that storms are coming, and so do winds from the southeast. This is because winds blow into lows, never away from them. If we have an east or southeast wind and the air becomes "muggy," we suspect that a low is coming from the west. If clouds appear and become thicker and lower, we forecast snow or rain.

Now suppose that the weather has been stormy, with dark nimbo-stratus clouds in the sky. The wind has blown from the east, too — but it slows down, shifts, and then starts to come from the northwest. This tells us that a cold front is arriving. It may mean another short storm, but then it will bring clear weather.

As lows and highs travel past, we often wonder where to find them. One good way is to stand with your back to the wind and spread your arms straight out sidewise. The nearest low is a little way ahead of the direction in which your left hand points, and the nearest high is in the opposite direction.

Does that seem puzzling? Try it when the wind is in the southeast. Your right hand will point toward the northeast, but the high will not be quite as far north. Your left hand will point southwest, and the nearest low will be in that direction, but not quite so far south. Watch the clouds and winds to make sure whether to predict a storm.

We know how to tell whether air is humid — put ice water into a glass and see how many droplets form on it. If the weather outdoors is hotter than 90 degrees above zero, put a thermometer into the glass. If droplets form while the water is warmer than 70 degrees, thunderstorms will probably come in a few hours.

Another easy way to make sure that air is humid is to open the refrigerator. On dry days there is almost no "steam," which really is droplets of water that form in the chilly air. On humid days a little cloud will appear in front of the refrigerator.

Clouds are the best guides to use in making our own forecasts. Their meaning is told on pages 46 to 56 and in the description of fronts. But remember: the kinds of clouds mean less than the way they change. Watch the clouds if you want to find out what kind of weather is coming.

A *corona* (ko roe' na) is a circle of light which we see around the sun or moon when it shines through clouds. If a corona becomes smaller hour after hour, it means that droplets in clouds are growing so large that rain is almost sure to fall. But when the corona grows larger it shows that droplets are evaporating, and the weather probably will clear.

A thick coat of dew in the morning is a good sign that the day will be clear. Dew falls when the ground cools rapidly because the air high above it is dry. But when the air is very humid or clouds cover the sky, the ground does not cool so much and dew does not form.

About the poorest way to predict the weather is to use cheap "guides" or "indicators" that are given away as prizes or sold for a few cents. Most of these things work only by accident, when their predictions happen to fit the weather that actually comes. You can do much better than that by watching the winds and clouds.